LITERATURE & WRITING WORKSHOP

EXPLORING BIOGRAPHIES

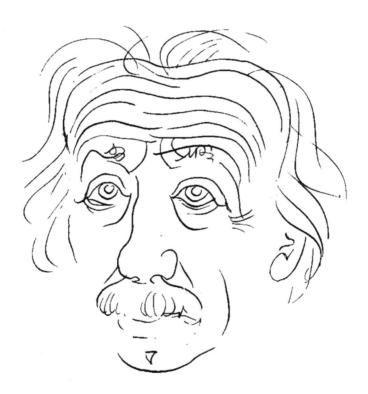

TEACHER'S SOURCEBOOK

SCHOLASTIC INC.

EDITORIAL—*Editor:* Deborah Jerome-Cohen • *Associate Editor:* Wendy Murray • *Literature Research:* Eileen Burke, Teresa Cullen • *Sourcebook Writer:* Janet Cassidy

ART—*Art Directors:* Tony DeLuna and Patricia Isaza • *Computer Design:* Robin D'Amato

EDITORIAL ADMINISTRATION—*Editor-in-Chief:* Terry Cooper • *Editorial Design Director:* Vincent Ceci

PUBLISHING—*Vice President, Professional Publishing:* Claudia Cohl • *Vice President, Circulation and Marketing:* Stephen Bernard • *Marketing Director:* Jane Fisher • *Marketing Manager:* Melanie Seto • *Fulfillment Manager:* Joan Marcelynas • *Business Manager:* Beth Polcari • *Promotion Design Director:* Dale Moyer • *Promotion Manager:* Carol Skolnick • *Manager, Product Manufacturing:* Laurie Giannelli.

ADVISORY BOARD—Joyce Baltas, National Language Arts Consultant, Scholastic • Karen D'Angelo Bromley, Professor, the School of Education and Human Development, Binghamton University, Binghamton, NY • Eileen Burke, Chairperson, the Reading and Language Department, Trenton State University, Trenton, NJ • Doris Dillon, Primary Language Arts Resource Teacher, San Jose Unified School District, San Jose, CA • Theresa Hancock, 5th grade teacher, Brookside Elementary School, Worthington, OH • Suzanne Houghton, 4th grade teacher, Grace Church School, New York, NY • Lynn Parsons, 5th grade teacher, Stratham Memorial School, Stratham, NH

ART CREDITS–Cover: Design by Patricia Isaza, photograph courtesy of The Bettmann Archive. Title Page: Illustration by Josef Scharl. Page 12: Copyright © 1989 by Universal Press Syndicate. Reprinted by permission. Page 41: Illustration by Rick Geary.

PHOTO CREDITS–Page 6: Benjamin Franklin: Courtesy of the New York Public Library Picture Collection. Page 7: Abraham Lincoln: U.S. Bureau of Engraving and Printing. Page 9: Abraham Lincoln: AP/Wide World portrait by Garner. Page 20: Albert Einstein: AP/Wide World.

ISBN 0-590-49295-0

PHILOSOPHY

When a child begins to write a story with "Once upon a time" and tells of magic spells or characters who live happily ever after as a reward for their kindness or heroism, it's clear that the inspiration is coming from the storybooks the child has read or heard. Recent studies on the reading-writing connection have pointed to a simple, important truth: Children who are exposed to literature incorporate ideas and literary structures into the writing of their own stories.

This connection between reading and writing has inspired a unique program: The Scholastic Literature & Writing Workshop provides everything you need to get students excited about literature and to get them to use what they read as models for what they write.

In focusing on the elements of a genre or a kind of writing, and in giving students practice with these elements, you will be making students aware that language and literature have structures—structures that can be understood. The Literature & Writing Workshop helps students deepen their appreciation for literature and writing by giving them high-quality works and the precise tools for building their own narratives.

Developed by teachers for teachers, the Literature & Writing Workshop reflects the latest thinking in promoting literacy: The program is inquiry-based, child-centered, and provides plenty of opportunity for students to make choices and follow their own particular enthusiasms. Many activities in the program are also designed to foster a cooperative sharing of knowledge and ideas.

PROGRAM MANAGEMENT

Devoting three to four weeks to Exploring Biographies will allow students to become truly immersed in biographies and their structure. This sourcebook will help students analyze what they read, react to what they learn, and use their new knowledge to create their own biographies.

On the next page you will find a chart showing you how the program is organized.

For each story in the anthology, you will find teaching strategies for introducing and analyzing the selection, discussion ideas, and literature connections. All the activities in the sourcebook can be done individually or as a group. The three selections are arranged in order of difficulty—from the straightforward "Nellie Bly: Remarkable Story of the Successful Female Reporter" to the more complex "George Washington Carver."

Literature & Writing Workshop

INTRODUCING THE GENRE

- calling on prior knowledge
- defining the genre
- special genre terms

SELECTION 1

- background info, teaching tips
- prereading, post-reading activities and responses
- exploring a literary device

SELECTION 2

- background info, teaching tips
- prereading, post-reading activities and responses
- exploring a literary device

SELECTION 3

- background info, teaching tips
- prereading, post-reading activities and responses
- exploring a literary device

ANALYZING THE THREE SELECTIONS

- compare / contrast story elements
- refine the definition of the genre

EXTENDING THE READING

- outside reading in the genre
- cross-curricular activities

WRITING AN ORIGINAL GENRE PIECE

- brainstorming and research
- developing specific elements
- outlining, drafting, conferencing
- revising and publishing

END OF UNIT EVALUATION

- student self-evaluation
- teacher checklist

Dear Parent:

The Scholastic Literature & Writing Workshop is a unique program designed to introduce your child to different writing styles and to help your child develop as an analytical, appreciative reader and capable writer.

Exploring Biographies is part of a 16-unit series that includes such literary forms as biography, humor, and poetry. As your child works with the Biography unit, he or she will read three biographies, analyze them, and use what has been learned to create his or her own biography of a relative or other person.

Here are a few ways to enhance your child's study of biographies:

- Child psychologists stress the importance of heroes to child development. Talk with your child about his or her heroes. What makes those heroes admirable in your child's eyes? Has the person contributed to the betterment of mankind, shown great courage or great character, or worked toward some significant achievement? Is this the kind of person your child would like to be? Why?

- Discuss biographies you have read with your child. What famous persons have you admired? What is there about the person's life that has caused you to relate to it?

- If there is a nearby site associated with a well-known person, such as Lincoln's home in Springfield, Illinois, or Eleanor Roosevelt's home in Hyde Park, New York, try to arrange a visit with your child. Talk with him or her ahead of time about the person and why he or she is famous. Try to get a biography of the person that you and your child could read together.

- Talk to your child about interesting people in your own family. While you might not have anyone famous in your family tree, sharing stories about your own memories or grandparents or other relatives gives children a sense of heritage and belonging. If you have a family photo album, share it with your child. Plan trips to your own family's "historical sites," too.

Happy reading!

About Biographies

Biographies are popular with adults and children alike. Their appeal lies in the fact that they help make the past come alive, and they satisfy readers' curiosity about the lives of the famous. Biography offers children the excitement and drama of fiction, while giving them the added satisfaction of knowing the events and people described are real. A good biography presents the facts about an individual's life, and also makes an attempt to interpret those facts, explaining the person's feelings and motivations.

Early biographies tended to idealize their subjects. During the Middle Ages, for example, biography was really hagiography, the "lives of the saints," which focused on the subjects' virtues and miracle-working. During the Renaissance, the emphasis shifted from religious subjects to military leaders and other secular figures, but the portraits were rarely well-rounded. During the 1600s and 1700s, biography grew in popularity and biographers' techniques became more sophisticated. Biographers took a more scholarly approach by using a variety of research materials, avoiding hearsay, and checking their facts. They also began paying more attention to literary style, probably due to the growing popularity of the novel. James Boswell's *The Life of Samuel Johnson*, written in 1791, is considered by many scholars the finest biography of all time.

During the 1800s most English-language biographers tried to imitate Boswell's style. However, most biographies of this period were incomplete accounts because writers still tended to take an entirely uncritical approach to their subjects. American biographies of the 1800s followed the model of their English counterparts. Biographies of Revolutionary War heroes tended to glorify their subjects. George Washington was particularly subject to attempts at "canonization." Mason Locke Weem's *Life of George Washington* is one example. Jared Sparks, another Washington biographer, even "improved" the wording of Washington's letters.

After 1900, influenced by the writings of Sigmund Freud, biographers attempted to incorporate the new sci-

Leonardo da Vinci

ence of psychology. Freud's own work, *Leonardo da Vinci* (1910) explained the personality of its subject in psychoanalytical terms. Other biographies that make good use of psychological theories of behavior are Leon Edel's 5-volume *Henry James* (1953-1974), and *Thomas Jefferson: An Intimate History* by Fawn M. Brodie (1974).

Biographies written for children reflected social attitudes toward children. Books for children have often been religious and social tools. From the seventeenth through the nineteenth centuries, children's biographies reflected the Puritan, and later the Victorian, emphasis on duty to God and parents. Children were presented with stories of the saints, and of virtuous boys and girls who died early and went to Heaven. When, by the mid-1800s, the cultural emphasis shifted to realizing the American dream, children were presented with political leaders as heroes to emulate.

In the twentieth century, psychologists emphasized the vulnerability of children. Biographers continued to protect children from the subjects' vices, and even from their failures. Biographies still did not explore motives, and most biographies for children also ignored the subject's death.

Benjamin Franklin

The first significant "modern" biographies for children date from the 1930s. One of the first was Sandburg's *Abe Lincoln Grows Up*, adapted from Sandburg's *The Prairie Years*. James Daugherty, writing in the 1930s and 1940s, produced several powerful biographies, among them *Daniel Boone*, *Poor Richard*, and *Abraham Lincoln*.

Other significant contributions to the field were Ingri and Edgar

Parin d'Aulaire's picture-book biographies, including *Abraham Lincoln*, *Benjamin Franklin*, and *Columbus*.

In the 1950s author-illustrator Robert Lawson wrote several humorous fictionalized biographies using animal narrators. *Ben and Me* is the "true" story of Ben Franklin's life as told by the mouse who lived in Ben's fur hat.

It was not until the mid-1900s that the contributions of female and nonwhite Americans were regarded highly enough to be considered appropriate subjects for biography. Elizabeth Yates' *Amos Fortune, Free Man*, the story of a slave who bought his freedom, was the 1951 Newbery Medal winner.

During the late 1960s and 1970s, a new openness in children's fiction reflected changing social and family values. Hero worship gave way to a more realistic approach, with a fuller and more honest treatment of subjects. At the same time, more and more books were written about groups previously overlooked—women, Native Americans, African-Americans, and members of other minorities.

Biographies written for children now develop many sides of a subject's character, including their negative qualities. Jean Fritz writes delightful biographies that mix humor with fact and show the subjects as real people. Her biography of Patrick Henry, *Where Was Patrick Henry on the 29th of May?*, depicts the patriot as a practical joker who disliked school as a boy. Other Fritz biographies include *And Then What Happened, Paul Revere?* (1973), and *Bully For You, Teddy Roosevelt* (1990).

Theodore Roosevelt

F. N. Monjo has written portraits of famous American statesmen as told through the eyes of a son, grandson, or granddaughter. In *The One Bad Thing About Father*, Quentin Roosevelt describes life in the White House with his father, Theodore Roosevelt. Monjo purposely chooses to use a child narrator to limit the biography to those things a child would consider important and to avoid filling the biographies with more facts than a young reader wants to know. Al-though he uses fictionalized scenes and dialog, Monjo says his biographies are "about ninety-eight percent fact." At the end of each book the author helps the reader distinguish between fact and fiction by pointing out the parts he created.

While some authors use fictionalized scenes and invented dialog, Jean Fritz does not. Says Fritz, "…I try to present characters honestly, with their paradoxes and their complexities, their strengths and their weaknesses. To do this I involve myself in as much research as I would if I were writing biography for adults. Contrary to what I call 'old-fashioned' biography for children, I do not invent dialog. I use dialog only when I can document it. I do not think that children need facts dressed up in fictional trimmings. Indeed, children welcome hard, specific facts that bring characters to life—not only the important facts but those small vivid details that have a way of lighting up an event or a personality."

Biographies written for children today are often as well-documented as those written for adults. One such work is Russell Freedman's *Lincoln: A Photobiography*, the 1988 Newbery Medal winner. Freedman includes a listing of quotes from Lincoln's speeches, historical sites associated with Lincoln, and a bibliography of additional

Abraham Lincoln

sources. Virginia Hamilton's *Anthony Burns: The Defeat and Triumph of a Fugitive Slave* (1988) includes a listing of primary sources used by the author.

Children also enjoy reading about the writers and illustrators they have come to know through their books. Excellent autobiographies include Elizabeth Yates's *My Diary, My World*; *Self-Portrait: Margot Zemach*; and Disney artist Bill Peet's *Bill Peet: An Autobiography* (the 1990 Caldecott Medal winner). Jean Fritz wrote a fictionalized autobiography, *Homesick: My Own Story*. Beverly Cleary's *A Girl From Yamhill: A Memoir*, is more suitable for young adults, but younger readers of the "Ramona" series will enjoy the photographs of Cleary growing up.

Introducing Biographies

Here are a few biography-centered activities to help get your students involved in the study of biographies.

- Encourage children to make collections of items (print and nonprint) related to a person they are studying. The collection can consist of photos, drawings students have made of the subject, maps showing the person's travels, artifacts (such as a compass for Einstein), diagrams, dioramas, etc.

- Students reading the same biography could work together to build a collection. They could then share it with another group, inviting them to read the biography and examine the collection.

- Biography is an ideal way to study history. In addition to researching and writing reports on a particular era, student groups can create displays related to world events of that period. The display can include newspaper headlines, household tools used, fashions, song lyrics, and slang popular during the subject's lifetime.

- Develop a Biography Learning Center in your classroom. Provide biographies from the local or school library, and invite students to bring in their own books to share with the class. Also make available films, records, or tapes related to famous individuals.

Page 9: What Do You Know About Biographies?
Use this sheet with the entire class. Discuss the etymology of biography. (From the Greek roots, *bios*, meaning "life", and *graphia*, meaning "writing.") Have students list other words containing these two roots (biology, biologist, biopsy, biosphere, telegraph, autograph, photograph, phonograph, seismograph).

As students begin their study of biographies, you may wish to cover the following questions:

- How does a biographer find out about the subject's life? Where does the biographer get his/her information?

- How does the biographer decide which information to include in the biography? Should the biographer tell about the subject's faults or failures, or only the "good" things?

Page 10: A Biography Survey
Suggest students work as a team to take a survey of biographies in their school library or local public library. Then have them present the information to the class to analyze. Help students analyze the information they find. They may want to prepare a graph or chart to display their findings.

INTRODUCING BIOGRAPHIES

What do you know about...
BIOGRAPHIES?

Think about what you already know about biographies. Then work with a partner to answer the questions below.

The word biography comes from two Greek root words, *bios* and *graphia*. Look up biography in a dictionary that gives word histories. Write the meaning of the roots *bios* and *graphia*:

bios _____   *graphia* _____

1. What is a biography?_____

_____

2. Name someone whose biography you have read._____

3. Write something you learned about that person from reading about him or her.

_____

_____

4. Who is the person in this picture? _____

5. What do you know about this person? _____

6. What did this person accomplish?_____

_____

7. Why do we care about him today? _____

_____

_____

_____

8. What other people would you like to learn about? _____

_____

Name(s) _____

A Biography Survey

Work with a group to take this survey of biographies in your school or local library.

Count the number of biographies in your library. How many are there? _____

How many of the biographies are about people you've heard about? _____

Now analyze the kinds of biographies. How many do you find in each category?

White men _____   Presidents _____

African-Americans _____   Sports figures _____

Hispanics _____   Artists, musicians, writers _____

Other ethnic groups _____   TV or movie stars _____

Women _____   World leaders _____

Scientists _____   Other _____

Explorers _____

How many are written about people who lived before 1900? _____

How many are about people born in this century? _____

How many are about people still alive? _____

Who has the most biographies written about him or her? _____

_____

Which biographies seemed to have been borrowed from the library the most? _____

_____

Ask your librarian how the library decides what biographies to purchase. _____

_____

_____

NELLIE BLY: REMARKABLE STORY OF THE SUCCESSFUL FEMALE REPORTER

Introducing the Selection

Before reading "Nellie Bly," discuss with students what jobs were open to women one hundred years ago. Point out that a woman who had a career was unusual. You might discuss with students why women were expected to stay at home. The Victorians viewed women as wives and mothers. While women were revered and respected in these roles, they were also considered weaker than men and in need of protection, including protection from the business world's "harsh" realities. A woman who wanted a career was regarded as attempting to usurp man's place, and was considered unwomanly.

Page 12: Writing Conversation

To illustrate how the conventions of writing conversation make it easier to read, write out the words of the cartoon without quotation marks, indents, or words added to identify the speaker. (If this is done with a word processor, students can go back and add quotation marks, etc.)

You might also discuss how the writer can influence interpretation of a speaker's words. For instance, contrast "I don't like it," said Sam, with "I don't like it!" shouted Sam angrily.

Page 13: Preview and Predict

Use this sheet to help students preview the selection. What qualities do students think good journalists share with good biographers? In what ways are journalists and biographers both like detectives?

Page 14: Knowledge Web

Use this sheet for all three anthology selections.

Write the name of each biography subject in the center. The boxes around the web may be used after reading to summarize information about the subject. The sheet also can be use   .ing-reading exercise by children who find it helpful to take notes as they read.

Page 15: Responding to the Story

After students have completed this worksheet, you may want to repeat the activity as a whole-class exercise using chart paper or the chalkboard. You can extend the activity to include incidents that presented problems and challenges to Nellie and showed her character and beliefs. Students may also use the diagram to plan their own biographies.

Page 16: The Life and Times

Biographies can bring history to life for children. This activity can help students see the relationship between people's lives and the times in which they lived. When students are listing events in history, encourage them to focus on events related to Bly's life.

Page 17: Be a Reporter

This activity gives students a chance to practice their own reporting and writing skills. Bring in newspaper articles and help students analyze their structure. Have students note that the opening sentence, known as the lead, is very important. Students should also note that the opening paragraphs usually cover the questions Who, What, Where, When, Why, and How.

You might choose to display students' finished articles on a bulletin board.

SKILLS LESSON

Writing Conversation

Copyright © 1989 by Universal Press Syndicate. Reprinted by permission.

It's easy to know what a character is saying in a cartoon, because the words are written in the balloon over the character's head.

Look at the dialog in the cartoon above. Then notice how we would write the same dialog, or conversation, if we were writing a story:

"I think we've got enough information now, don't you?" asked Calvin.
"All we have is one 'fact' you made up," answered Hobbes.

The words that appear in the cartoon balloon are supposed to be the words the characters are speaking. When we write the same words in a story or a book, we show this by surrounding them by quotation marks. Notice that the question mark is inside the quotation marks. The period at the end of Hobbes' statement is replaced by a comma, because we have added the words that tell who is speaking.

In the cartoon we can see who is saying the words. But in writing conversation we usually add words like *asked Calvin* and *answered Hobbes* so the reader can tell who is speaking.

Practice writing conversation by writing out the rest of the cartoon. Or find a cartoon of your own and write it as conversation.

NELLIE BLY

Preview and Predict

"Nellie Bly" is the story of Elizabeth Cochrane, a famous newswoman who lived about one hundred years ago. Before you read about her, look at the paragraph below. Then get together with a partner and complete the questions.

> Today there are women dentists and women doctors, as well as women firefighters and women police officers. In fact, women work at all kinds of jobs. But one hundred years ago in this country, it was expected that if you were a girl you would probably get married when you grew up and then stay home to raise your family. A double standard held that it was acceptable for poor women to work in factories, as dressmakers, or on farms with their husbands. But a "lady" who didn't marry or who needed money was limited to being a schoolteacher or governess. The idea of women building careers because they wanted interesting work was unheard of.

1. List some other jobs that women do today that were not open to women one hundred years ago. _____
_____

2. Elizabeth Cochrane wanted to be a reporter. What skills do you think it takes to be a good reporter? _____
_____

3. A pioneer is someone who is first at something, like the first person to travel in space. Why would it be difficult to be a pioneer? _____
_____

4. What kind of personal qualities would it take to be the first to do something?_____
_____
_____

5. What kind of person do you think Elizabeth was? _____
_____
_____

NELLIE BLY

Knowledge Web

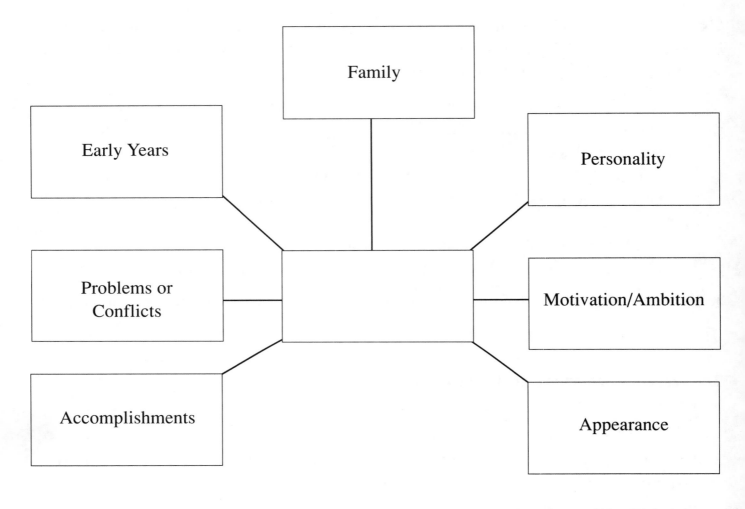

Now use the web to think of another way to tell the story of the subject's life. Write down your ideas and then share them with a partner.

_____

_____

_____

_____

_____

NELLIE BLY

Responding to the Story

Think of the biography you have just read. Write two or three of the most interesting things you learned about Nellie Bly. _____

_____

_____

_____

_____

A biographer cannot tell everything about the subject's life, and therefore makes choices about which events or incidents to include. The biographer chooses the events that best illustrate what he or she thinks the subject is like.

With your partner, think of words that describe Nellie and write them in the circles of the web. Then go back to the selection. Find episodes or incidents that show the quality you listed. (For example, if you decide Nellie was ambitious, find an incident that shows this.) Write notes about the incident around the circle.

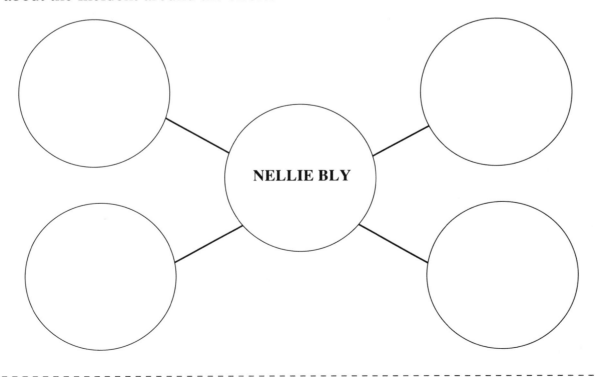

Name(s) _____

NELLIE BLY

Life and Times

Nellie Bly was born more than one hundred years ago. What was happening in the country and the world during her lifetime? Work with a group. Use encyclopedias and history textbooks to discover what events in history occurred during Nellie's life. Use the chart below to show your findings.

Events in Nellie's Life   Events in History

_____ 1864 _____

_____ 1870 _____

_____ 1875 _____

_____ 1880 _____

_____ 1885 _____

_____ 1890 _____

_____ 1895 _____

_____ 1900 _____

_____ 1905 _____

_____ 1910 _____

_____ 1915 _____

NELLIE BLY

Writing Warm-Up:
Be a Reporter

Try your own skill at being a reporter. Write about something or someone at your school.

First, your story should be newsworthy. That is, it should be about something or someone special. It might be an interview with the science fair winner, the lead in the school play, a new teacher, or someone with an unusual hobby. You might interview the coach about the team's chances this year, or the cafeteria manager about new menu ideas.

Take notes. Then write your article as a newspaper reporter might.

Next, trade articles with a partner. Now be the editor! Edit your partner's article. Then work together to create headlines for your articles. You might want to work with a group of your classmates to make a class newspaper from your news stories.

Use the space below to jot down ideas for news stories, or to take notes.

_____
_____
_____
_____
_____
_____
_____
_____
_____
_____
_____
_____
_____

ALBERT EINSTEIN

Introducing the Selection

Before reading "Albert Einstein," discuss with students what it means to say that someone is "an Einstein," or display a photograph or drawing of Einstein. Your students may be able to identify him, as his image is one of the most recognizable of the twentieth century. Explain that Albert Einstein is considered one of the greatest scientists of all time.

Page 19: Skills Page

Before beginning this activity, you may wish to read aloud vividly written passages from a biography you enjoy. Then have students discuss why they think the writing in the passage is/is not lively.

Page 20: Preview and Predict

Use this sheet to help students assess what they already know about Albert Einstein. Explain that Einstein's research made it possible for scientists to develop the atomic bomb used in World War II. Point out that this was ironic, because all his life Einstein was opposed to war. He had only encouraged research on the bomb because he feared that Germany might develop the weapon first.

A victim of anti-Semitism, Einstein also supported Zionism and was offered the Presidency of the newly-formed state of Israel in 1952. He declined, saying he was not suited for the position.

Page 21: Think and Respond

Depending on your group's abilities, you may wish to do this as a teacher-directed activity. Give students time to respond orally to the selection, telling what they learned about Albert Einstein.

Page 22: Responding to the Story

Use this page to help students analyze how biographers show important influences in a subject's life. The compass, the violin, and the math books Albert received when young affected his life. Students can use the web to take notes on who gave these gifts, and what effect they had on Einstein.

This is a good place to introduce the idea of point of view and interpretation in biography. The biographer develops a point of view about the subject and then selects, shapes, and arranges the material based on that viewpoint. If we were to rewrite Einstein's biography to focus on the people who influenced him, we would shift the point of view.

Page 23: Writing Warm-Up

Have students use the diagram to take notes on people they think have been important to their own lives. (You may wish to introduce the term *autobiography* at this point.) Be sure they understand that the "gift" someone gave does not have to be tangible—it could be a skill taught, or something inherited, such as musical talent.

Mini–Study: Fictionalized Biography

Expand students' understanding of point of view by reading aloud a fictionalized biography written from another point of view. Two good choices are Robert Lawson's *Ben and Me* (the story of Ben Franklin narrated by a mouse really responsible for Franklin's inventions), or *Mr. Revere and I* (the story of Paul Revere's famous ride as told by his horse). Children could then read independently the fictionalized biographies by F. N. Monjo (see Bibliography). These are stories of famous men such as Lincoln, Jefferson, and Franklin, as they might have been told by a son, granddaughter, or other child. Students may then be challenged to use this technique themselves.

Using Lively Language

Why are some biographies exciting to read, while others are boring? It's all in the language the writer uses. Biographies that have lots of details are more interesting to read. Details add colorful "brushstrokes" of information about the events of a person's life.

Read the following passages about Supreme Court Justice Sandra Day O'Connor's childhood on a cattle ranch in the southwest. Which passage do you like best?

1. During her first years on the isolated ranch, Sandra had no other children to play with, but she found plenty of things to entertain her. There was a world of deserts and canyons to explore and all sorts of wild animals to get to know. Many of the creatures of the desert became Sandra's pets. Sandra recalled: "One day my father was on a roundup and he found a tiny baby bobcat that had been abandoned by its mother. He put it in his jacket and brought it home. We kept him for years, and he grew up to be a great big gray cat."

    from *Sandra Day O'Connor* by Norman Macht, Chelsea House Publishers, 1992.

2. During her childhood on the ranch, Sandra played by herself because there were no other children to play with. She explored the land and got to know the animals that lived there. Once, her father found a bobcat and brought him home. It became a pet.

The first selection has many details that make it more interesting than the second one. The details tell more about *what* is happening, *who* the people are, and *what* the bobcat was.

Using Colorful Quotes

Look at the first passage from the Sandra Day O'Connor biography. Notice that many of the interesting details come from a quote from Sandra herself. The quote not only gives you a picture of the baby bobcat, but tells you about Sandra's father. What details show this?

_____

Using Adjectives

Look at the first selection. Can you find all the adjectives? List them here. _____

_____

How do they help make the biography more interesting to read? _____

_____

ALBERT EINSTEIN

Preview and Predict

1. Do you know this man? His name is Albert Einstein. Before you begin reading his biography, take a moment to think of what you already know about him. Write facts you know about Albert Einstein on the lines below. _____

_____

_____

_____

_____

_____

_____

2. Einstein worked in a branch of science called physics. Look up the word physics in a dictionary, or find a chapter about physics in your science book. What kinds of things do scientists study in physics? _____

_____

_____

Einstein is famous for an idea called the "theory of relativity." It changed the way that scientists thought about time, space, light, gravity, motion, and energy. Einstein's ideas paved the way for scientists to work with nuclear energy.

3. What is something that nuclear energy is used for today? _____

_____

4. What would you like to learn about Albert Einstein?_____

_____

_____

_____

_____

ALBERT EINSTEIN

Think and Respond

Now get together with a group and discuss the biography you just read. What did you learn about Albert Einstein? What kind of person was he? Is he someone you admire? What problems did he have in his life? What were his goals? What did he accomplish?

1. Write something you would like to remember about Albert Einstein.

_____

_____

_____

_____

_____

_____

2. Do you think the biography explained clearly why Einstein is important?

_____

_____

_____

_____

_____

3. What else would you like to know about Einstein that the biography does not tell?

_____

_____

_____

_____

_____

_____

ALBERT EINSTEIN

Responding to the Story

In the biography of Einstein we learned that several people gave him gifts that influenced his life. (For example, his Uncle Jake's gift of the algebra book opened a new world for Albert.) Fill in the circles on the web with the names of other people in Albert's life. Then use the space around the circles to write notes about what these people gave Albert, and how their gifts affected his life. (Remember: Gifts are not always objects.)

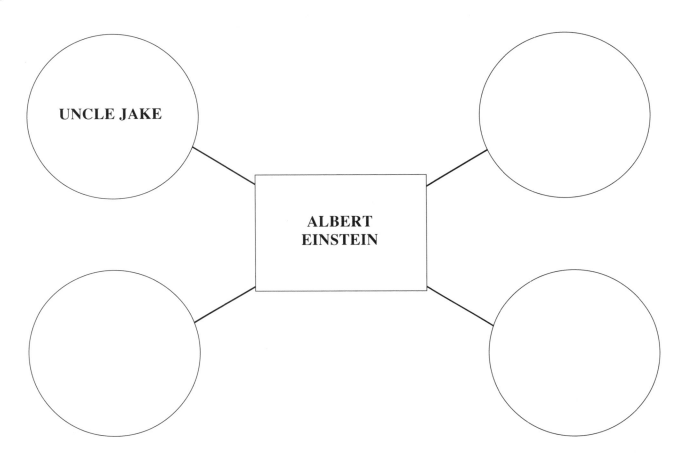

Now use the diagram and the notes you wrote to retell to a partner the story of how these people influenced Albert.

ALBERT EINSTEIN

Writing Warm-Up:
From Your Own Life

Now practice writing biography. Use the subject you know best—yourself! Think about one or two people who have been important to you. Perhaps it was someone who gave you a gift that opened new worlds to you. Or it might have been someone you admire and hope to be like someday.

Use the web below to organize your thoughts. Write your name in the center. Write the names of people who have been important to you in the circles. (You can add more circles if you like.) Take notes around the circles. Then use your notes to write about these people's influence on your life.

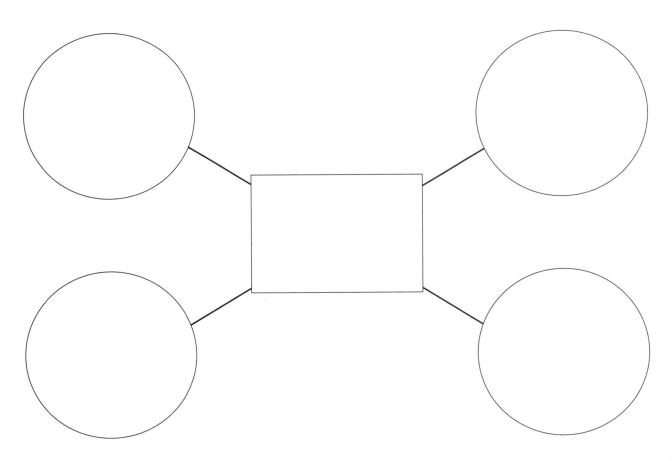

GEORGE WASHINGTON CARVER

Introducing the Selection
Point out to students that just as opportunities for women were limited over one hundred years ago, so were opportunities for African-Americans. Explain that it's important to remember these limitations in understanding both the strength of George Washington Carver and the significance of his achievement.

Page 25: Good Beginnings, Good Endings
Encourage students to find and share favorite beginning or ending paragraphs of biographies and other books they have enjoyed. You might create a bulletin board that shows good beginning sentences.

Remind students that the end of a biography should tie together the thoughts they are trying to communicate about the subject, and include some sort of summary of the subject's accomplishments. Have students find and share favorite endings.

Page 26: Preview and Predict
Invite students to discuss what they know about life for African-Americans during the period after the Civil War through the first half of this century. What opportunities were there for a boy like Carver to get an education?

Page 27: Responding to the Selection
Allow students time to give their personal responses to the biography. Discuss with students the problems and challenges Carver faced. Would a white boy growing up during the same period have faced the same challenges? Invite students to speculate how Carver's life might have been different if he had been born one hundred years later.

Page 28: The Life and Times
This activity helps students compare the events in Carver's personal life with events in history. Help them focus on historical events that impacted on Carver's life, such as the Civil War and the 15th Amendment. You may want to lead students in a discussion of how current events might be shaping their lives.

Then have students go back to the biography to note details the biographer included that give the reader a feeling for the time period.

Page 29: Getting to Know the Subject
Before beginning this sheet, discuss with students what kind of person Carver was. Ask them to support their opinion with evidence from the biography. Then allow them to complete the worksheet.

Page 30: Writing Warm-up: A Character Sketch
Before assigning this activity, you may wish to read aloud a character description or character-revealing incident from another biography.

Expanding
Encourage students to read other biographies of Carver (see Bibliography). You may want to read one of the more advanced biographies aloud to the class. Help students compare the author's approach with that used in the anthology. Also note any new or contradictory information learned.

SKILLS LESSON

Good Beginnings, Good Endings

From Beginning

Every story needs a beginning that will pull readers into the story. A strong beginning makes readers want to keep reading.

Consider this beginning to Russell Freedman's *Lincoln: A Photobiography.* After opening the chapter with a quotation from one of Lincoln's letters in which Lincoln describes himself, the biographer says:

> "Lincoln wasn't the sort of man who could lose himself in a crowd. After all, he stood six feet four inches tall, and to top it off, he wore a high silk hat."

After giving us this vivid picture of Lincoln, Freedman then discusses how people of his time regarded Lincoln and how we view him today.

Look at the biographies in your anthology. How does each begin? Now check other biographies you have read. Find an opening sentence or paragraph you really like and write it here. _____

_____

_____

_____

_____

To End

In telling about the life of a subject, a biographer includes many facts. A good ending should sum up what has been learned. It should tell the reader why the subject is worth remembering.

Read the last paragraph of each biography in your anthology. What do these paragraphs do that make them good endings?

_____

_____

_____

_____

GEORGE WASHINGTON CARVER

Preview and Predict

Before reading the biography of George Washington Carver, work with a partner to complete the questions below.

1. Look up Carver's name in a dictionary or encyclopedia. Find the dates he lived. Write them here. _____

2. What was happening in our country the year George Washington Carver was born?

_____

_____

_____

3. Think about what it might have been like for young George to be growing up at that time in our country. What problems do you think he might have had? _____

_____

_____

_____

_____

GEORGE WASHINGTON CARVER

Responding to the Selection

1. What was your reaction to George Washington Carver? Write something you learned about Carver's life that you didn't know before. _____

_____

_____

_____

2. What were some of the problems or obstacles Carver had to overcome? _____

_____

_____

_____

_____

3. What did you find most interesting about Carver's life? _____

_____

_____

_____

_____

4. Now trade papers with a partner and read your partner's reactions. Write your response to your partner's comments below. _____

_____

_____

_____

_____

_____

_____

_____

_____

GEORGE WASHINGTON CARVER

Life and Times

George Washington Carver lived during an exciting and difficult time in this country. Work with a group. Use encyclopedias and history textbooks to discover what historical events occurred during this time. Concentrate on the events that had an impact on Carver's life. Use the chart below to show your findings.

Events in Carver's Life		Events in History
_____	1864	_____
_____	1870	_____
_____	1875	_____
_____	1880	_____
_____	1885	_____
_____	1890	_____
_____	1895	_____
_____	1900	_____
_____	1905	_____
_____	1910	_____
_____	1915	_____

Continue the chart on the other side of this page.

GEORGE WASHINGTON CARVER

Getting to Know the Subject

A good biographer does not simply tell the reader about the subject. Instead, the writer includes incidents that illustrate the subject's character or beliefs.

Go back to the selection. Find incidents the biographer used to illustrate Carver's character. Use the web below to take notes on them.

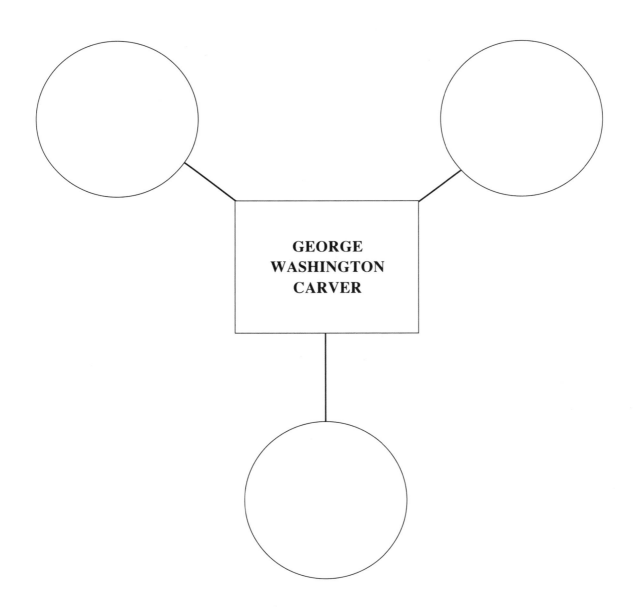

GEORGE WASHINGTON CARVER

GEORGE WASHINGTON CARVER

Writing Warm-Up:
A Character Sketch

Think about someone you know well. How would you describe him or her? What incidents could you relate that would illustrate the person's character? Use the web below to take notes on two or three incidents that help show your subject's personality or character. Then use your notes to write a brief character sketch of the person.

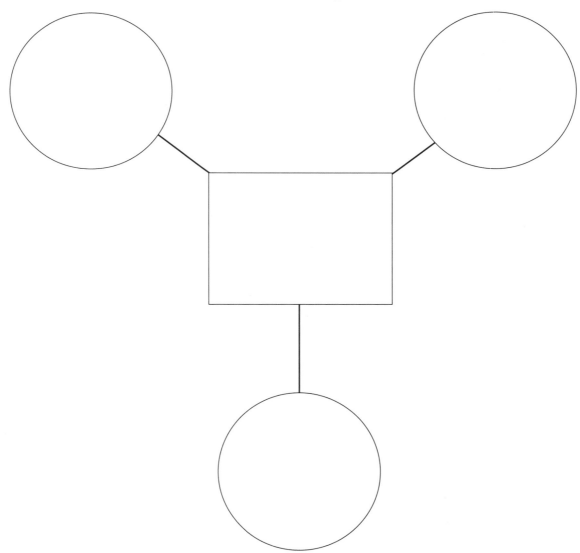

Analyzing Biographies

This section is designed to encourage students to discover more about biographies by comparing and contrasting the three selections they have read.

Page 32: Comparing the Subjects

This activity helps students focus on the subjects' places in history and compare the information included in the anthology. Depending on your group's abilities, you may wish to begin this sheet as a teacher-directed activity. After the chart is completed, help students analyze the information included in each biography. Did the writer relate the subject's entire life, or concentrate on one part of the subject's life? Did the biographer emphasize the problems the subject faced? Did the biographer include motivations or reasons the subject acted the way he or she did?

Page 33: A Good Beginning

This sheet will help students analyze the beginnings of the three biographies in the anthology. Have them review the texts, as well as the opening paragraphs, of other biographies they may have read. In each case, discuss why students think the writer chose to begin the biography the way he or she did.

Page 34: Talk It Up

Discuss with students how they think the biographer knew what Nellie Bly said to Joseph Pulitzer during this conversation, since there were no tape recorders in those days. Explain to students that biographers often do not know the exact words that the subject used. Writers sometimes invent conversation, based on what the subject wrote in letters or diaries. Some authors, such as F. N. Monjo, tell their readers outright when they have invented scenes or dialog. Some provide clues, such as "perhaps he thought," or "he might have said." Others, such as Jean Fritz, refuse to use quotation marks unless there is a source for the quote.

Point out to students that there are drawbacks to using conversation. A biographer can put his own interpretation on what the subject may have said and can actually distort the speaker's intentions. You may wish to review the mechanics of writing conversation at this point, using page 12.

Page 35: On Your Own

Make many kinds of biographies available to students for use in the classroom. You may wish to set aside a short time each day for a "book talk" in which volunteers tell the group about the biographies they are reading. Invite them to read aloud sections they find especially interesting, or to share any interesting bits of information they have learned. Talk to your students about the biographies you have read, too. Encourage students to read more than one biography of the same person so they can contrast the approaches and information given. They may find it helpful to use a Venn diagram to compare the information.

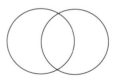

Discuss with students why they may sometimes find different or contradictory information in biographies about the same person. Where can they go to check any discrepancies they find?

Another idea is to have students read several biographies by the same author, such as Jean Fritz, Milton Meltzer, F. N. Monjo, or Robert Quackenbush.

ANALYZING THE SELECTIONS

Comparing the Subjects

Think about the three persons whose biographies you have read. Work with a partner to complete the chart below to compare them. You may want to refer to the knowledge web (page 14) you did for each subject.

Person	Lifespan	Occupation	Problems/ challenges	Motivations	Accomplishments

ANALYZING THE SELECTIONS

A Good Beginning

A good biography, like any good "story," needs an interesting beginning. But there are different ways to begin.

1. Look back at the three selections you have read. Reread the first few paragraphs of each. Think about how each writer began the biography. Which beginning do you find the most interesting? Why? _____

_____

_____

_____

2. Which selection begins with the subject as an adult, ready to start a career? _____

_____

_____

3. Which begins with an exciting incident soon after the subject's birth? _____

_____

4. Which begins with a description of the city where the subject lived? _____

_____

5. What other way could you begin a biography? _____

_____

_____

_____

_____

_____

_____

_____

_____

_____

_____

Talk It Up

Here is one way the writer might have told about Nellie Bly's idea for a story on Blackwell's Island.

> Nellie told Pulitzer that she had a good idea for a new story. Since she wanted to learn what Blackwell's Island for the insane was really like, she would pretend she was insane and get sent there.

Now read the way this incident is told in "Nellie Bly."

> She told Pulitzer, "I have a good idea for a new story. I'll find out what Blackwell's Island for the insane is really like from the inside."
>
> "How?" said Mr. Pulitzer.
>
> Nellie gulped. "I'll have to pretend that I'm insane, too."

Most readers like to read dialog. It helps make a story more interesting. Dialog can make a biography more interesting, too. The reader feels like an eyewitness to the subject's life.

Practice writing dialog. Think of something that happened to you that could be told through conversation, and write about it. Then trade papers with a partner. Have a writing conference to work on ways you can both make your dialogs or conversations more lively.

_____

_____

_____

_____

_____

_____

_____

_____

_____

_____

ANALYZING THE SELECTIONS

On Your Own

1. Read several other biographies. What was the most interesting one you read? Write the title and author here. _____

_____

(If the subject isn't clear from the title, write his or her name here.)_____

_____

2. What made it a good biography? _____

_____

3. Do you share any characteristics with the subject? Which ones? _____

_____

_____

_____

_____

4. Would you like to be like this person? Explain why or why not._____

_____

_____

_____

_____

5. Did reading about this person teach you anything about your own life? _____

_____

_____

_____

_____

_____

Across the Curriculum

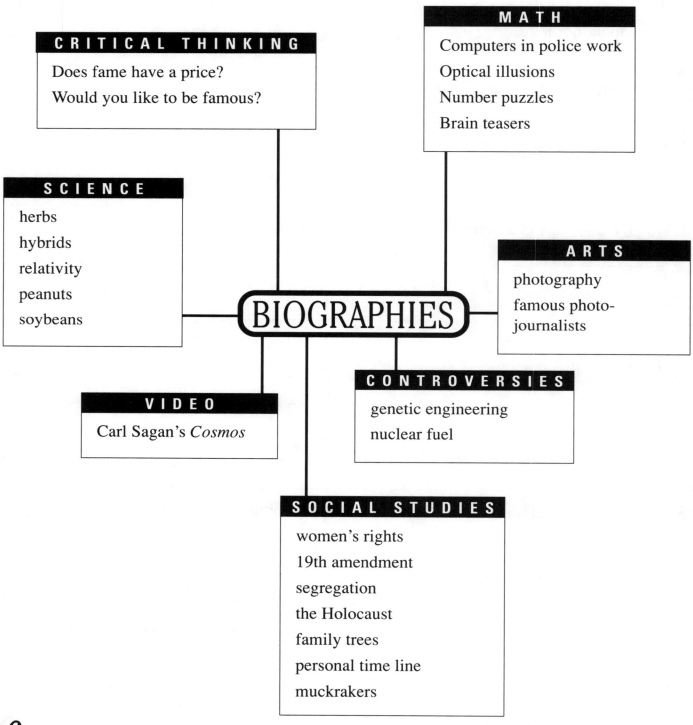

CRITICAL THINKING

Does fame have a price?

Would you like to be famous?

MATH

Computers in police work

Optical illusions

Number puzzles

Brain teasers

SCIENCE

herbs

hybrids

relativity

peanuts

soybeans

ARTS

photography

famous photo-journalists

BIOGRAPHIES

VIDEO

Carl Sagan's *Cosmos*

CONTROVERSIES

genetic engineering

nuclear fuel

SOCIAL STUDIES

women's rights

19th amendment

segregation

the Holocaust

family trees

personal time line

muckrakers

Recommended Biographies for Students

Apfel, Necia H. *It's All Relative: Einstein's Theory of Relativity*. Lothrop, 1981.

Blair, Gwenda. *Laura Ingalls Wilder*. Putnam, 1981. Easy-to-read biography of *Little House* author.

Bulla, Clyde Robert. *A Grain of Wheat: A Writer Begins*. Godine, 1985. The writer describes his early years on a Missouri farm.

Caruth, Ella Kaiser. *She Wanted to Read: The Story of Mary McLeod Bethune*. Illus. by Herbert McClure. Abingdon, 1966. Inspiring story of the 19th-century black educator.

Collins, David. *The Country Artist: A Story About Beatrix Potter*. Illustrated by Karen Ritz. Carolrhoda, 1989.

Collins, David. *To the Point: A Story About E. B. White*. Carolrhoda, 1989.

Greenfield, Eloise. *Mary McLeod Bethune*. Illus. by Jerry Pinkney. Harper, 1977.

Fisher, David E. *The Ideas of Einstein*. Holt, 1980. A basic explanation of the concept of relativity.

Freedman, Russell. *Lincoln: A Photobiography*. Clarion Books, 1987. Newbery Award winner.

Fritz, Jean. *What's the Big Idea, Ben Franklin?* Illus. by Margot Tomes. Putnam, 1976. Franklin's life told in this author's clever, lively manner.

Fritz, Jean. *Homesick: My Own Story*. Putnam, 1982. In this fictionalized autobiography, the author tells of her childhood in China.

Gish, Lillian, as told to Selma Lanes. *An Actor's Life For Me!* Viking, 1987.

Goodsell, Jane. *Eleanor Roosevelt*. Crowell, 1970.

Haskins, James. *James Van Der Zee: The Picture Takin' Man*. Dodd, 1979. Portrait of the Harlem photographer.

Jacobs, William Jay. *Eleanor Roosevelt: A Life of Happiness and Tears*. Putnam, 1983.

Latham, Jean Lee. *Carry On, Mr. Bowditch*. Houghton Mifflin, 1955. Fictionalized biography of the great American navigator. Newbery Medal winner.

Lawson, Robert. *Ben and Me*. Little, Brown, 1939. Ben Franklin's life told through the eyes of a mouse who knew him well.

Lawson, Robert. *Mr. Revere and I*. Little, Brown, 1953.

Lee, Betsy. *Charles Eastman, The Story of an American Indian*. Dillon, 1979. Eastman was a doctor, writer, and activist for rights of Native Americans.

McGovern, Ann. *The Secret Soldier: The Story of Deborah Sampson*. Scholastic, 1975. The story of the girl who, disguised as a man, served in the Continental Army.

Meltzer, Milton. *Langston Hughes: A Biography*. Harper, 1968.

Meltzer, Milton. *Dorothea Lange: Life Through the Camera*. Viking Kestrel, 1985. Photographs by Dorothea Lange. Balanced portrait of the famed photographer.

Monjo, F. N. *Me and Willie and Pa: The Story of Abraham Lincoln and His Son Tad*. Simon & Schuster, 1973.

Monjo, F. N. *Letters to Horseface*. Viking, 1975. Letters from Wolfgang Amadeus Mozart to his sister.

Peet, Bill. *Bill Peet: An Autobiography*. Houghton Mifflin, 1989. Caldecott Honor Book.

Quackenbush, Robert. *Don't You Dare Shoot That Bear! A Story of Theodore Roosevelt*. Illus. by author. Prentice, 1984. A biography that mixes humor and fact.

Stanley, Diane. *Peter the Great*. Four Winds Press, 1986.

Wilson, Dorothy Clarke. *I Will Be a Doctor! The Story of America's First Woman Physician*. Abingdon, 1983.

Writing a Biography

For a warm-up to the final biography writing project, suggest students practice interviewing one another, or school personnel, and write mini-biographies. Have students work in a group to brainstorm a list of questions to ask subjects. If possible, use a camcorder to videotape students as they practice their interviewing skills on one another. Play back the tape so kids can see where they need to

Page 39: Choosing a Subject
Having students write about a living person forces them to do their own research from primary sources and organize information in their own way, rather than rewrite another author's ideas. Writing about a grandparent or other older relative can help students develop a sense of time and history. Students could also write "ancestor stories" about deceased relatives, gathering information from living relatives who knew the subject. They might tape their interviews as part of an oral history project.

Suggest they look through the family photo album, or ask other family members for ideas, in order to "sleuth out" an interesting relative or other subject.

Page 41: Snapshot Biography
A snapshot biography is the easiest approach to biography. For younger or less advanced students, it may represent the finished product. For more advanced students, the snapshot approach can form an outline for a longer work. Students may also enjoy dramatizing the events shown in the snapshot biography, and creating dialog to accompany them.

Page 42: Two Ways To Go
This sheet presents two ways to plan the presentation of facts in a biography, and gives an alternative to chronological order. It helps the student confront the issue of time in a biography.

Page 43: Have an Argument
The "thesis statement" approach is the most challenging approach to biography given here. Students decide on a position and then present facts from the person's life to defend the position. This approach challenges them to shape arguments from their own interpretations of the facts.

Page 44: Write a Draft
Give students plenty of time to write their biographies. If they have trouble beginning at the beginning, suggest they start with an interesting part of the subject's life. They can go back to work on the beginning later.

Page 45: Writing Conference
Students may prefer to conference about their writing in small groups rather than with a partner. This gives them the added benefit of several points of view. Remind students to be constructive in their criticism.

Page 46: Revise and Publish
Give students time to evaluate the suggestions they have received, and to make revisions in their work. Help the group develop ways to share the biographies when completed. One idea is to use the information in the biographies as the basis of a "This Is Your Life" series. Students might also enjoy dressing up as the subjects of their biographies and improvising scenes in which two subjects meet.

WRITING A BIOGRAPHY

Choosing a Subject

Now it's your turn to think about writing a biography. For your subject, choose someone you know well: a relative, or someone in your town who has an interesting life.

Or, you might want to write about someone in your family who is no longer living, such as a grandparent who has died. Then you can base your biography on your own memories, as well as memories of people still living who knew the person.

1. Write the names of three or four people whose biography you might want to write.

_____

_____

_____

_____

_____

_____

_____

_____

2. Choose one person from the list. Whom will you talk to for information about this person? What other information sources will you use? _____

_____

_____

_____

_____

_____

_____

WRITING A BIOGRAPHY

Researching Your Subject

A good biography is based on solid research. You can gather information in lots of ways. Here's a checklist you can use:

- Interview your subject.
- Interview others who know (or knew) him or her.
- Check high school yearbooks.
- Examine the old family photo album.
- Read diaries or letters the person wrote. (But get permission first!)
- Check the newspaper: Maybe your subject's name was in the paper. Did he or she ever: receive an award? _____ get elected president of the local Elks Club or Rotary?_____ play on a high school football team?_____ get married?_____

(Your local library may have old issues of newspapers on microfilm. Ask your librarian.)

When you interview someone, remember these tips:

- Explain what you're doing and make an appointment.
- Get the person talking—it takes time for the memory to start rolling. As people talk they'll start remembering more and more.
- Use a tape recorder, or take notes. You won't remember everything.
- Have your questions ready in advance, but follow up an interesting sideline if one develops.
- Ask memory–jogging questions like:
  - How did it happen that you were born where you were?
  - Did your father have a car when you were young?
  - When and where did you meet your husband (wife)?
  - What was high school like when you went?
  - What were your ambitions when you wre my age?
  - Did you ever want to have a different job than you have now?
  - Who were some of the people who were most important to you when you were a teenager? A young adult? Who influenced you the most?
  - What was your biggest disappointment? Your toughest time? Your happiest time?
- Avoid questions that can be answered by just "yes" or "no." Remember to thank the person when the interview is over.

WRITING A BIOGRAPHY

Snapshot Biography

One way to organize your information is to create a snapshot biography. Here's how:

- First make a list of events in the person's life that you want to include. Then close your eyes and imagine what the event might have looked like.

- Draw each event. Include as much detail as you can.

- Write a description of what is happening in each drawing.

- Use posterboard. Arrange the drawings in a circle in chronological order, going clockwise.

- In the center, write a summary of the person's life. To write your summary, think about the following: How are the events in the snapshots similar? How would you describe the person's life?

Nellie went around the world in less than 80 days.

She was offered a job! She wrote about factories and slums, using the name Nellie Bly.

Nellie wrote a story about Blackwell Island insane asylum. Her story got her a job on the *World*.

Elizabeth worked as a reporter gathering facts to help her father.

Nellie went to New York to see Joseph Pulitzer.

NELLIE BLY

Elizabeth wrote an answer to an editorial in the Pittsburgh *Dispatch*.

WRITING A BIOGRAPHY

Two Ways to Go

Once you've gathered all your information, it's time to plan your biography. How will you tell your subject's story?

One way is to begin at the beginning, telling about the person in chronological, or time order. You would then begin at birth, and tell what happened in order until the person's death (or up to now, if your subject is a living person).

Your biography would look like this:

Birth	Event 1	Event 2	Event 3	etc.	Death

Or you can approach things another way. Suppose you are writing about your grandfather, who owned a restaurant in your town. Through the restaurant, he made enough money to send his two children to college. In doing your research you find out he came over from Italy when he was sixteen, with two dollars in his pocket! How did he do it?

Instead of starting your story with your grandfather's birth, you could start by telling about your grandfather as an adult. You could show him at the peak of his career as a successful restaurant owner, and THEN go back and show the things that helped him become a success.

Your biography would look like this:

Event 1	Event 2	Birth	More Events	Death

To help plan your biography, first make a time line of events in your subject's life. You could list them below, or write each event on a separate 3 x 5 file card.

_____

_____

_____

_____

WRITING A BIOGRAPHY

Have an Argument

Here's another way to write a biography. Suppose you're writing about that grandfather who owned the restaurant. As you gather research, the question comes up: Was there anything in your grandfather's early life that prepared him to be a success in the restaurant business?

Instead of simply telling the events of your grandfather's life in chronological order, you could use the biography to answer the question. You could even argue both sides before presenting your conclusion.

	Did Grandfather's early life prepare him to be a success in the restaurant business?	
YES Tell what experiences prepared him. Why was it not surprising he was a success?		**NO** Tell why he was unprepared. Why was it surprising that he was a success?

To write this kind of biography, first think of an important question to ask yourself about your subject. (A question that can be answered with YES or NO is easiest.) Write the question:

_____

_____

Then choose a position. Think of all the arguments you can that support your position. List them below. (Use the back of this sheet if you need more room.) _____

_____

_____

_____

_____

Start your biography with a description of your subject at the high point of his/her life or career. Then present the question and your arguments. Finally, write a conclusion to your biography.

WRITING A BIOGRAPHY

Write a Draft

Write the first draft of your biography. As you write, keep these questions in mind:

- What are the important events in my subject's life?_____

_____

- What details can I add that will make events come to life?_____

_____

- What do I think of the subject? How can I use the facts I've learned to illustrate what I think?_____

- What do I think was the subject's most important contribution?_____

_____

When your draft is finished, read it over. Use this checklist to think about your work. Then make whatever changes you need.

The Biography:

- Does the biography have a beginning that will grab the reader's attention?
- Did I tell the important events in the subject's life?
- Did I follow an order that makes sense?
- Does the subject "come alive"?
- Did I include interesting details?
- Did I give the reader a picture of the time period?

Mechanics:

- Do all sentences have correct punctuation?
- Did I write conversation correctly?
- Did I use capital letters where needed?
- Did I start a new paragraph for each new idea, and indent paragraphs?
- Did I check the spelling of any words I'm not sure of?

WRITING A BIOGRAPHY

Writing Conference

Get together with a partner and exchange biographies. Read your partner's biography carefully. Use the checklist from "Write a Draft" to evaluate your partner's work:

1. Think about what is good about your partner's biography. What do you like about it? What is the most interesting part? Write your comments here:

_____

_____

_____

_____

_____

_____

_____

_____

_____

2. What could your partner change or add that would improve the biography? Write your suggestions below:

_____

_____

_____

_____

_____

_____

_____

Then get together and discuss each other's biographies. Remember to make helpful suggestions.

WRITING A BIOGRAPHY

Revise and Publish

Reread your draft:

Think about the suggestions your partner made. Which ones will you use? What ideas of your own do you have to improve your biography? Do you want to rewrite any parts?

Write your corrections in the margin, or between the lines. Don't worry if the draft is messy. You will copy it over later.

Proofread:

Carefully reread your entire biography, word for word. Correct any mistakes, or any misspelled words. Change or add details to make the writing more interesting. Try reading parts out loud to see if they sound right to you.

Use these proofreading marks:

⌐   indent

chicago capitalize

to home go move a word

⌒   take something out

⊙   add a period

⋏   insert something

Publish:

Think of a title for your biography. Then make a final, neat copy in your best handwriting, or use a typewriter or word processor. Think of how you want to illustrate your biography.

Get together with a group and think of ways to share your biographies. You might want to make a class display, have a class read–aloud, or publish a class anthology. You may want to prepare a copy of your biography to give to the subject.

Write some ways you could share your biographies. _____

_____

_____

BIOGRAPHIES

End of Unit: Student Self-Evaluation

Make a mark on the line to chart your response:

I enjoyed working in this unit

0 ————————————————————5————————————————————10

not at all   somewhat   a great deal

My work on this unit was

0 ————————————————————5————————————————————10

not as good as my usual   about average for me   my best ever

In working on this unit, I most enjoyed

_____ working on my own.   _____ working with a partner.   _____ working in a group.

The biography I most enjoyed reading was _____

because_____

_____

Something new I learned about one of the people we read about was _____

_____

_____

The best thing about working on this unit was _____

_____

_____

The thing I liked least about working on this unit was_____

_____

What I would like to do better as a reader is_____

_____

Something I learned from reading biographies was _____

_____

Something I learned from writing a biography was _____

_____

One way I can improve my writing is_____

End of Unit: Teacher's Checklist

Student _____

Reading Comprehension	Mastery					Unsatisfactory
identifies main ideas	5	4	3	2	1	0
recalls details	5	4	3	2	1	0
makes inferences	5	4	3	2	1	0
recognizes structures of biography	5	4	3	2	1	0
understands subject's place in history	5	4	3	2	1	0

The Writing Process	Mastery					Unsatisfactory
self-selects topics	5	4	3	2	1	0
researches information	5	4	3	2	1	0
understands biographies have a structure	5	4	3	2	1	0
understands chronological order	5	4	3	2	1	0
revises writing	5	4	3	2	1	0
follows ideas to completion	5	4	3	2	1	0
shares writing	5	4	3	2	1	0

Mechanics	Mastery					Unsatisfactory
uses capitalization	5	4	3	2	1	0
uses end punctuation	5	4	3	2	1	0
uses quotation marks	5	4	3	2	1	0
uses correct grammar	5	4	3	2	1	0